Sales Operations for Small Businesses

How To Scale your Business with Sales Strategies and Tactics

by

I0482051

WW Chee

Books by
WW Chee

The Sales Operations Handbook

Getting the Most Out of your CRM

Sales Operations for Small Businesses

Managing the Sales Pipeline

Table of Contents

Legal Notes

Introduction

The sales operations was pioneered by Xerox in the 1970's and these days companies like Microsoft, Google, LinkedIn, Samsung, Thomson Reuters, and Verizon have their own sales operations teams.

While Sales Operations is gaining traction in corporations, a common question I hear being asked is "is this applicable to smaller businesses?" The answer is a definite yes! After all, what is good for the goose is also good for the gander.

The function may be known by a variety of other names such as "sales support", "sales effectiveness", "sales backend", "sales administration", or a number of other related titles. The purpose of these roles are all the same: To improve the sales of the company, without adding more headcount.

The sales operations function achieves this by improving the efficiency and effectiveness of existing salespeople. This is done through implementing a sales strategy, and sound processes that work for your organization. The core concept of sales operations, "method, enablement, analysis", still holds true. It is only the scale of it which differs; small and medium businesses still face the same challenge of sales as larger corporations, and will see benefits in adopting a structured approach to sales.

This book explores how to effectively implement the principles of sales operations and set up the function in your small medium enterprises to help you scale your business. Following the structure of "method, enablement, analysis", I will outline the strategies and mindsets to adopt, then go over how to implement these in your business, and follow with the analysis that will sustain this approach of sales operations.

If you are running a small business or a start up and are looking to scale your business without increasing your sales headcount, this book is for you.

Chapter 1. What is Sales Operations?

First the basics. Sales operations is the function of removing inefficiencies in sales. This chapter is an excerpt from my first book "The Sales Operations Handbook". If you would like to better understand the basics of sales operations, it is a good starting point.

The Role of Sales Operations

Wikipedia defines sales operations is a set of business activities and processes that help a sales organization run effectively, efficiently and in support of business strategies and business objectives.

Since the early 2000's, more and more companies are forming sales operations departments within their organizations to establish sales processes, monitor sales metrics, and implement the usage of sales tools.

However, with more tools in use, it is estimated that salespeople spend roughly a third of their time selling and the other two-thirds on non-selling activities. It is the sales operations department's job to improve that ratio.

A good sales operations team will have an impact on productivity and increase the effectiveness of salespeople by reducing the time they spend on non-sales tasks, allowing them to spend more time selling. Studies have found that there is a direct correlation between the focus on sales operations and sales target achievements.

While the details may differ from company to company, the scope of the Sales Operations team fall into three primary functions, and two secondary functions.

Primary Functions

1. Method
2. Enablement
3. Analysis

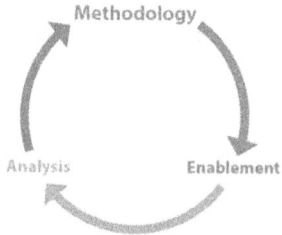

The three primary functions are effectively a cycle.

Methodology is the backbone of the sales organization and determines how the organization sells to its customers. A good methodology that is well implemented will allow the sales organization to have a standardized approach to sales, with a standardized language.

When the method is decided, the salespeople need to be enabled. Enablement is about selecting the right tools, communicating the decisions to the salespeople, and training the salespeople on the usage of the tools, or the purpose of the process.

After the enablement comes the Analysis. KPIs should be defined clearly, and tracked, either via the tools, or from the other departments like operations, or finance. Good analysis should measure the success of the salespeople, and the effectiveness of processes, training, campaigns and all sales activities.

From there it feeds back into the cycle, and sales operations can determine the value of the method and recommend changes to the processes or plans.

Secondary Functions

1. Administration
2. Sales Tools

The secondary functions of the sales operations team are an offshoot of the primary functions. Administrative tasks such as contract filing, order processing, pricing, and upkeep of customer records. This should also be in line with the method, and enablement efforts.

The selection, maintenance, and administration of sales tools also fall under secondary responsibilities. It is usually for the sales operations team to perform data uploads to the tools and provide login details or password resets (or at least arrange with the vendor for the above).

Chapter 2. Sales Operations for the Small Business

The reason small and medium businesses have difficulty scaling is that sales is seldom approached from an operational perspective. It is common that growth in sales is linear and proportional to the number of salespeople, as there is very little understanding of data. As a result, processes are largely left up to individual sales representatives and any forecasting or planning is often not aligned with customer buying habits. Enablement is usually limited to mentoring, and sales tools are also limited at best.

The efficiency of a sales operations function however is a comparative advantage. This is the main reason that small medium businesses need to dedicate resources to a sales operations role. This is the only way to scale sales without increasing the headcount; by making your existing salespeople more efficient. Very often this may be an additional responsibility for someone a management role, or someone managing sales and marketing support.

When the sales operations function is covered well, ideally results are measured accurately and sales is managed according to those results. Prospecting and lead generation is done more efficiently, leading to better quality of leads. Sales is improved by having processes in place, leading to a more consistent approach across all sales representatives.

The bottom line is that there must be someone focusing on understanding and streamlining the sales processes. This will help the company to grow efficiently, showing results in the bottom line. Among the list of objectives for the sales operations functions, these three are key things to understand in order to operationalize your sales team:

Understand the Necessity of Sales Operations

Due to limited resources, sales and marketing functions in small businesses are usually covered by the business owner and a small group of salespeople. Very often this handful of people will have limited marketing and selling knowledge due to the breath of activities that they cover. This translates to ineffectiveness in sales and marketing activities

Hiring for a sales operations role in early stages is becoming more common, and is seen to be a necessity for long term success. This role is designed to steer the sales team by understanding the strategies and tactics required, as well as adjusting them for the organization. Removing the inefficiencies by planning sales makes each individual sales representative more effective as they are guided along to grow the business.

Address Issues Early

A very common mindset with small medium businesses is waiting to address problems due to limited resources. Issues like inconsistencies in reporting or forecasting, differences in individual sales techniques, and availability of sales and marketing collateral are often seen as something that is lower on priority.

However, these little issues can quickly grow, and its impact is amplified the more the business grows. Eventually, this may end up inhibiting the growth of the company. Addressing issues early sets the process and culture for the organization, allowing the business to scale and scale correctly.

Apply Strategy Universally Across All Functions

As the effectiveness of the sales team affects the entire business, sales operations has an effect on the entire organization as well. In large corporations, it is commonplace to have sales operations sit in on strategy meetings alongside business operations, strategic consultants, and C-level executives.

In small medium enterprises, this means that the role may be expanded to include other strategic functions as well. Consolidating these functions means that the team performing this role has better oversight on how each function of the business affects the rest, allowing better coordination and synergy between these functions. A spend on tools can be better optimized for multiple functions, providing more value for a greater number of people.

Ultimately sales efficiency improves, marketing results improves, operations becomes optimized, and finance is aware of the developments.

When to Make Your First Sales Operations Hire

Spoiler: Do it as soon as possible.

As the number of salespeople in your business increases, your client database expands accordingly as sales goes up. Very likely this will mean that the data in the company will suffer in quality and integrity. It is common to find double entries, missing data, or even incorrect data.

With the growth of the sales force, it is almost guaranteed that each salesperson will have their own method of sales. From prospecting, to qualification, to product demonstration, to negotiation, and finally closing the sale each individual will have inconsistencies in their performance and outcomes.

Having someone responsible for sales operations aims to address these issues and more, so hiring one as soon as possible will set the ground right for both new and existing sales staff before culture and habits set in. Fixing a lack of operationalized sales could take months or even years, and cost the company millions as reported in an article on Medium in 2016.

3 Characteristics of a Good Sales Operations Hire

When making the first sales operations hire the list of responsibilities can seem daunting. Sales operations needs to handle sales tools (primarily CRM), including the evaluation and purchase. He or she also has the responsibility of generating reports and pulling insights from those reports, turning data into recommendations for management. Sales related activities such as training, on-boarding, creating and updating collateral, supporting RFPs (Requests for Proposals) and RFQs (Request for Quotations) all fall under the purview of sales operations as well. In short, everything a good sales manager or director would do aside from facing the customer could fall under sales operations.

The trick then is to prioritize. As a single person can be overwhelmed by the mountain of responsibilities, effort has to be made where there will be the biggest impact on the top line. To do that, these are the qualities to look for when hiring for sales operations:

Analytical & Methodical

Sales operations frequently deals with huge amounts of data. In a small medium business, this may not be the case. However, having an analytical and methodical mindset ensure that the data is presented in a way that will scale with the business. Sales operations started out as a reporting function, and while it has grown to so much more in recent years, the roots of this are still relevant today.

Being methodical in approach to sales ensures that processes are easily followed, which feeds into consistency in performance.

Ability to Think Strategically and Tactically

Having the big picture is important to sales operations, as the role requires planning and coordination with other strategic parts of the business like marketing, operations, and finance. Being able to think strategically allows sales operations to pace the sales department along the rest of the organization.

Tactics is the ability to put sales strategy into action. Sales operations is responsible for creating and maintaining collateral, coaching and training salespeople, and very often reviewing individual engagement plans. Having a tactical mindset will help in ensuring that each individual part drives the strategy forward while being pragmatic to the task at hand.

Excellent Communication Skills

Sales operations may be a "back office" role, and seldom do sales operations staff end up facing a client. However, this role interacts with other departments frequently, and is also required to guide salespeople as a mentor or coach, or sometimes as a strategist to the sales department.

Having excellent communication skills translates the data, reports, and presentation decks into something of value to each individual regardless of which department he or she is from.

This is what differentiates an average sales operations person from a good one. They represent the sales team to the rest of the business, and vice versa; this ensures that salespeople understand business objectives in a way relevant to them, and leadership has the insight on sales to make informed business decisions.

Chapter 3. Sales Operations Strategies

A new sales operations team needs to align their focus with the business and sales objectives. It is important to set clear objectives that are aligned with the rest of the business and then work along those lines staying on track to achieve those objectives.

A roadmap for sales operations is helpful when starting out; to understand what objectives need to be set, and ensure that objectives are being met in a systematic manner.

Understand Your Starting Point

Before making any decisions it is important to understand the state of things as they stand. This can be done by reviewing the material and data available, as well as talking with the salespeople. In particular, take note of the following:

1. The current state of sales

    Gathering data from sales, finance, and marketing to understand the current state of sales. This includes the volume of sales, the frequency of sales, the list of clients, and the rate of retention. Analyzing this data would be a great starting point from generating insight, showing the possible avenues where sales operations can make an impact. Also this analysis is useful to measure the effect of changes made, ensuring that any tactics implemented are in line with overall strategy.

2. The profile of clients

Understanding the client profile is important to segment customers. This helps to tailor marketing messages, sales collateral, and specialize salespeople. The client profile also provides understanding on the characteristics of clients, which would factor into consideration when designing sales processes, or engagement plans.

It is common for businesses to segregate customers by country, region, or industry and measure the performance of sales in each of these segments as different territories have different challenges or approaches.

3. The processes salespeople use when engaging customers

Understanding the current sales processes will help in finding out the commonalities between individual salespeople as well as their differences in strategies. The reasoning behind this would help in building a standardized process for the businesses. Matching this to individual sales data might also help in understanding where the difference in performance stems from.

4. The tools and material available to salespeople

As sales operations is usually the curator of sales collateral, and manages sales tools, it would be sensible to take stock of this. Collateral can then be standardized and then made available to all salespeople so the entire sales team can leverage on the best of what is available.

Understanding what tools are available as well as how and why they are used will pay off when streamlining the sales processes later on. Remember that these tools are made available so as to enable and benefit salespeople; if a tool does not achieve this goal it may make sense to repurpose or discard it.

Develop Processes & Policies

Processes and policies are important to help salespeople understand the common activities that need to be performed, when to perform these activities, and most importantly the steps required to perform these activities. Documenting and enforcing these processes ensures a consistent standard to which the activity is performed, especially when bringing on people new to the task or the organization.

The next logical step then, is to develop processes and policies for sales and sales operations.

Most obvious among processes would be sales processes, which is how a salesperson would manage a sales engagement with a prospect. This guides the salesperson through the entire sale from planning to qualification all the way to closing the deal. As this is an important topic, it deserves a chapter on its own and is covered in Chapter 4.

Aside from the sales processes, the other processes and policies that need to be developed for sales and sales operations are:

1. Lead qualification

   As the business grows, leads will start to pour in. Qualification becomes more important as the number of leads grow as bad leads will take up time that could be spent instead on good leads.

Understanding the client profile and the competition landscape will help to build the criteria needed to qualify leads.

2. Account/performance review

   As salespeople perform their jobs, it will be important to review the performance of accounts as well as their individual performance. The former to look for opportunities to up-sell or cross-sell, and the latter to ensure that salespeople are performing to the best of their abilities (or take corrective action such as training if they are not).

3. On boarding

   When new hires are made, having a process to onboard them quickly is essential to build their capabilities and get them productive. A good on boarding process will smoothen the transition into the role, and help the new hires adapt to the company's culture. In short, a good on boarding process will reduce turnover.

   A report by Aberdeen Group found that of companies that had an on boarding process:
   - 66% report better assimilation of new hires into company culture
   - 62% report higher time-to-productivity ratios
   - 54% report higher employee engagement

4. RFP/RFQ

Request for Proposals (RFPs) and Request for Quotations (RFQs) can be time consuming to write, and each RFP has unique requirements from others. The first step of the process is to decide if the RFP or RFQ should be responded to; this could be due to the volume, scope, or other factors of the request. Understanding which requests to respond to will increase the efficiency of the sales team, and increase the likelihood of a win.

If the business chooses the respond, the importance of a process is immediately apparent. It allows the sales team to effectively respond to RFPs and ensure that all requirements are met, and the business uses this opportunity to best showcase their capability.

Developing templates and pre generated responses will help cut down the time spent on replying to RFPs and RFQs, and it is commonplace in most organizations. These will usually be adapted as needed to each request that comes in.

5. <u>Social media</u>

It is impossible to ignore social media in this day and age. Regardless of which industry or who your target market is, there is an appropriate social media platform to use to reach out and connect with your audience. With a reach in the millions, it can be a useful tool to generate leads, demonstrate thought leadership, promote your business, and interact with your customers. On the flip side, if handled poorly, social media can be a PR disaster. This is why it is important to have a policy for social media to ensure that messages and posts are in line with the image and messaging of the business.

Selling over social media is also gaining in popularity for certain industries, with tools that link sales web pages to social media. Leads are also generated in this way, and having processes to qualify and follow up with these leads are necessary to ensure that these clients are not lost.

6. Data collection

Data is the lifeblood of sales operations. Without it, efficiency and progress cannot be measured. Collecting data therefore is important to ensure that reports can be generated, and analysis can be done in a timely manner.

Sources of data can come from a variety of places, from other departments to sales tools. It is important to have a process for this so that sales operations can keep a pulse on things.

It should be also noted that consistency in processes ensures that the data collected is meaningful data. To get accurate insights, sales operations must make sure definitions and processes are synchronized across the sales organization. Having clear definitions (such as the phases of the sales process) across all aspects of sales will ensure that reports generated have data integrity. This will result in meaningful insights.

The above are just a few examples which may be used to tailor to your business needs. As each business operates differently, the importance of each policy or process and the exact details may vary.

Prepare the Organization

Once your processes are decided, plans need to be communicated to the rest of the organization. Stakeholders need to understand what sales operations intends to deliver, and what they can expect to happen. Management would be interested in the results, salespeople would want to know about how these processes would benefit them, and other departments would be concerned about how they need to adapt to support sales, or vice versa.

Of all groups of people sales operations would need to prepare, salespeople would be the main focus of this step. Enabling salespeople involves the people (training, mentoring, coaching, and guidance), as well as equipping them with the tools and technology to do their job effectively.

Training & Guidance

Training and guidance equips salespeople with the skills and knowledge to do their jobs effectively. This includes product training, sales process training, training on tools, market knowledge training and many others. Having salespeople prepared reduces the probably of losing a sale.

Tools & Technology

From Customer Relations Management (CRM) systems, to Configure Price Quote (CPQ) systems, to Digital Transaction Management systems, there is a huge list of possible tools with many different offerings for each tool. Further to that, tools will have their own features, capabilities, and compatibilities.

Remember that tools are intended to make salespeople more effective. Tools should be selected for features that add value to the salespeople, either by easing their workload, saving time, or giving them a competitive edge of some sort.

Above all, remember that these features are only useful if they actually are pragmatic and used by salespeople.

The other aspect to this are sales collateral. Sales operations is usually the curator of such resources, and it is the responsibility of sales operations to keep them updated and disseminate them to salespeople. Collateral includes things such as product catalogues, presentation decks, sales and demonstration scripts, and white papers.

Make Tweaks for Improvement

The emphasis on sales operations is all about efficiency, and a part of that is constant improvement. As data is gathered, more insights can be gained which can be translated into business decisions. It is through this that the effectiveness of the sales operations team can really shine through.

There are three main areas that come to mind where data can make a difference. They are Win/Loss Analysis, Compensation, and Forecasting.

Win/Loss Analysis Review

Win/Loss reports will help to identify and analyze all the opportunities the sales team have won and lost within a time frame. This will help sales operations to monitor and measure the win rate over time by identifying the exact number of opportunities that the sales team has lost or won. This report will also help to identify the changes in the win rate and how it may look when filtered across various segments such as by product or by region. In addition, it will also track if the changes implemented in the sales team or the sales process is affecting win rates.

Analyzing win/loss reports involve data cohort that involves collecting certain data points and then closely keeping track of this group over time. The data can be sorted and tracked by time period or can be grouped by other dimensions such as customer, employee or lead source. Running these reports with different dimensions will give different views of the effectiveness of various factors in closing a sale.

Sales Incentives

When choosing the metric to measure success and reward salespeople on, note that some metrics are leading indicators, and others are lagging indicators. The former being predictions of future success, and the latter being a measurement of past achievements.

While it is common to reward salespeople on past achievements such as meeting their quotas, rewarding salespeople on leading indicators can set your organization up for future success.

Incentives can be also be paid out for gaining market share, acquiring new clients, maintaining a healthy sales pipeline, or any other metric that sales operations would like to emphasize the importance of.

<u>Forecasting</u>

Sales operations are essential in producing reports and analysis which drive recommendations. By using predictive models, the sales operations department can help take an active role in closing the gap between expected and actual sales performance.

Accurate sales forecasts allow companies to make informed business decisions, such as product launches, headcount needs, cash flow, and other resource allocations.

As the business expands, sales forecasting becomes a more important benchmark for the health of the company. It is easy to measure the success of a business by looking at its batting average on hitting its sales forecasts. If the business projects high sales in the 3rd quarter but only achieved 50% profitability, this is an indicator that the business is performing poorly and the management has no understanding of its capacity to hit sales targets. In attracting new investors for private businesses, sales forecasting could be used to project the possible ROI.

With accurate sales forecasting, a business can benefit from high efficiency, cost savings, increased profits and better customer service.

Pitfalls to Avoid

By the very nature of their function sales operations does not often get the spotlight the same way salespeople do. Coming from the origins of sales administration and data analysis, sales operations still maintains many of these functions to this day. That is the main pitfall for the sales operations function:

Not Breaking Out of an Administrative Role

While tasks like order management, territory collaboration, report generation are all important activities, there is risk of becoming a "dumping ground" for other administrative tasks if boundaries are not set.

"One-off" Tasks

Specialized analysis or reports that detract sales operations from their intended strategy, bogging them down with other priorities. This may be unavoidable when coming from upper management, but the value of these requests to the sales operations team should be carefully considered. If certain reports are worth having, then it may make sense to have this rolled up into the metrics that sales operations keeps track of.

Access to Data

While the main responsibility of sales operations is sales, it happens on occasion that data from other departments are needed. Data from HR such as term of service, average absenteeism rates, and compensation packages can be used to calculate the cost per sale, or productivity per headcount.

Finance may be needed to access revenue and profit, which sales may not have access to. In my experience, sales usually only has access to the total sale which leaves out any additional add-ons that may occur after the signing. This also neglects the SG&A (Selling, General, & Administrative costs).

The integrity and cleanliness of the data is just as important as the access to it. In   accurate   or incomplete numbers will result in a case of garbage in, garbage out affecting   the   credibility   of   sales operations.

Ideally the tasks that sales operations handles should be in line with the strategy of the department; these are the ones that develop the salespeople, track the processes, and measure the success of initiatives launched.

If sales operations loses sight of the strategy, or if management fails to keep the long term vision of sales operations in mind the function is doomed to be relegated to an administrative one.

If a gap or lack of alignment between the company's strategy and the focus of sales operations develops, the function of sales operations has failed. Therefore it is important to have a clear definition of the role and responsibilities of sales operations, and keep in mind its strategic value.

Chapter 4. Developing the Sales Processes

Of all the processes that sales operations would own, arguably the most important is the sales process. The Sales Management Association, a global, cross-industry professional organization for sales operations and sales management, found that companies with a structured sales process in place have an 18% higher revenue growth compared to companies without a structured sales process.

A well defined sales process aligns the sales of the business with the way customers would want to purchase the products or services offered by the company.

Consistency is key as it makes the process repeatable, giving clarity on what each salesperson needs to do to clinch a deal. It also serves to reinforce good habits of selling, which builds confidence and capability of those practicing the process.

As an added bonus, this consistency helps with evaluating performance and apply the same objective criteria to the rest of the sales team and manage them accordingly. By having an eye on the sales pipeline, understanding where each deal is on the stages of the sales process it is easier to forecast and plan for the long term.

Scaling Up

During the early stages of the business, it is likely that sales will be handled by the business owner, or a couple of salespeople with more enthusiasm than experience. Strategy and tactics do not factor into the concerns as much as building the client base or getting enough clients to stay in business.

However, as a business scales it cannot keep increasing the headcount for sales indefinitely. Moreover, the average output falls as the capability of individual varies more and more; not every salesperson is a self starter and some may be more inclined to maintaining existing accounts rather than winning new business. This may be a good thing if there are existing accounts that need to be serviced regularly by salespeople. However, it needs to be recognized and addressed otherwise these salespeople may not find their fit in the business.

Other factors such as familiarity with sales tools and job experience will also play a factor in individual performance. A fresh graduate may be less equipped to sell as compared to someone with more years of experience.

Therefore sales as a function needs to increase in efficiency, producing more per individual salesperson. Training and processes have to create an environment where succeeding in sales comes with the process; this should be the goal of sales operations.

Designing the Sales Process

The sales process should be a collection of best practices for moving the customer through each stage of the process and the desired outcome of each stage. Very often a win/loss analysis of deals feeds back into the modification and evolution of an organization's sales process. Therefore it is the responsibility of sales operations to ensure that these stages are clearly defined with the expected outcomes, roles involved, and tools that will facilitate the deal in each stage.

Having clearly defined stages means that the process is understood by all salespeople in the organization. This helps in knowing where each opportunity is in regards to the stages, how they should be managed, by whom, and which tools should be used.

Match the Selling Process to the Buying Process

Technology is equipping customers with better information about their needs, and proving more alternatives to solve their problems. This puts buyers in charge of the sale, and changes the way sales is carried out.

As product offerings are more easily available, it makes sense to align the sales process with how your customers move through their buying process. This reduces miscommunication, reduces frustration for both parties, and reduces the likelihood of deals stalling or dropping off.

Understanding the customer's profile or buyer persona, along with their motivations will help in defining the stages.

Define Sales Process Stages

Once the buying process is understood, the stages of the sales process should fall in to place. Each stage now needs to be clearly defined.

See the next section in this chapter for more details.

Streamline The Sales Process

As the process is tested in the field, the sales team will encounter obstacles. A pragmatic approach to sales should be the priority, and being knowledgeable and prepared is the best approach to this. Time is of the essence when pursuing an opportunity, so it is important for sales operations to adapt to feedback from salespeople.

If budget allows, sales tools can also be deployed to automate or reduce the time spent on certain tasks.

Defining Stages

Once the sales process is worked out, it can be broken down further into sales stages. Each stage should be clearly defined, and they should not overlap.

As mentioned above, the sales stages should align with the buying process, and should also include the following details:

- Activities that take place in each stage

- The people or functions that are involved in each stage

- The tools needed to perform the activities at each stage

- The criteria required to move to the next stage

Below is an example of a sales process with 6 stages. Note that these stages can be combined or further broken down to suit the needs of the business.

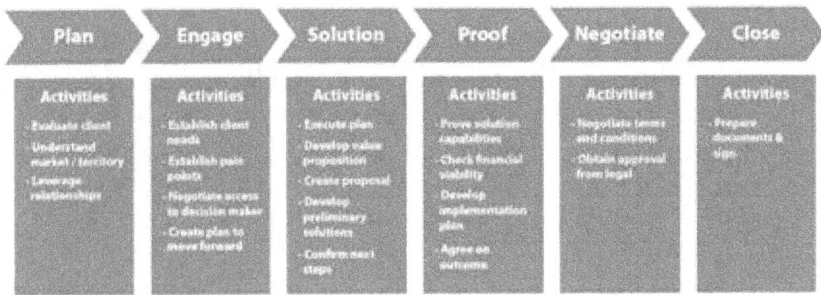

Stage 1: Plan

The first stage of any engagement is to understand the territory. The "Plan" stage is for the salesperson to evaluate the client and the market or industry the client is in. Understanding the stakeholders in the client's company can also lead to uncovering possible relationships to leverage.

Stage 2: Engage

The second stage is to engage the client, to establish their needs and to understand what the client perceives to be their pain points.

Establishing credibility also starts in this stage. The knowledge gained in phase 1 can be used here to demonstrate your company's capabilities.

Stage 3: Solution

This is the stage to develop the value proposition and preliminary solutions as a partner with the client. Building on the knowledge gained in the first 2 stages, these solutions should demonstrate the understanding of the client and the market/industry, and also address the client's pain points.

Stage 4: Proof

The "Proof" stage is about presenting the solution capabilities to the client, while checking on the viability of the solutions developed in the previous stage. An agreement on the outcome should be made in this stage and the client should have trust in the business and its ability to deliver on the solution.

Stage 5: Negotiate

This stage is when the terms of the deal are negotiated, and contracts are drawn out.

Stage 6: Close

The deal is complete, documents are signed. It's time to celebrate a job well done.

Adoption of the Sales Process

As processes are constantly being accessed, modified, and updated adoption of sales processes is a task that deserves looking into. Even the best processes will fail if not followed, and if no one is held accountable for implementing it.

It is the responsibility of the sales operations to prepare the salespeople as they adopt the sales process. This includes equipping salespeople with the appropriate tools such as manuals or playbooks, and supporting them by providing coaching and reinforcement after training.

Adoption is a process that takes time to be ingrained into the company culture. It takes time, effort, and a lot of reinforcement for it to take root, but once it does the value it provides will be difficult to dispute.

On that note, it is important to help salespeople understand how the process will help them improve their sales and therefore increase their earnings. Incentivizing salespeople on metrics directly related to the process is one way of doing this.

Having processes that avoids duplicate work, or reduces tedious tasks through tools is another way to sell the process to salespeople. Reporting is one such task that can be simplified. Instead of having multiple reports, a simple tool could take its place, where data could be stored on the system and reports generated from there.

Sales operations should look into periodically reviewing the process to keep it simple. Being pragmatic and reducing the complexity of stages to the minimum allows salespeople to adhere to the requirements. This ensures better consistency, without compromising on what is important.

Creating a Playbook

A playbook is one of the most important resources for salespeople as it details the sales process. It is created by the sales operations team, sometimes in conjunction with marketing.

It is usually launched in conjunction with the sales process, and is intended to enhance the awareness and educate all salespeople on the value of the sales process and tools at their disposal. It is a reference to ensure that the salespeople understand how the organization sells, and the role that they play, along with the expected outcomes in each stage of the sales process.

A good playbook should:

- Define the sales process
- Map the sales process to the customer's buying process
- Guide the engagement with a prospective customer
- State the tools, resources and outcome of each stage of the sales process
- Contain an explanation of resources and tools available to salespeople

In addition to the above, playbooks are also a good resource to help new hires acclimatize to the culture of the organization.

Sales Methodologies and the Small Business

If you are experienced in sales operations, you may be wondering "what about sales methodologies"?

Usually these methodologies are developed by vendors or consultants, with each having a unique view and approach to developing sales. Regardless of which methodology is chosen, the purpose of a sales methodology is to ensure that the business thinks about sales in the same way, and the people involved in a sale use a uniformed language.

As a small business, it may be impractical to hire a vendor to consult for your business and implement a sales methodology. However, the importance of having a uniformed approach and language should not be overlooked.

Chapter 5. Manage Your Pipeline to Move Deals Through

Pipeline management starts with designing the sales pipeline. The sales pipeline is a representation of the stages of a sales process, covered in Chapter 4. It is important to determine how sales operations will measure it, and how it will be used to drive individual performance from salespeople.

Pipeline management is a main responsibilities of sales operations, and good pipeline management can make a huge impact in sales performance. Keeping track of each opportunity in the pipeline can reveal gaps in sales.

According to Harvard Business Review companies with an effective pipeline management practice had a 15% increase in average growth over companies with ineffective pipeline management practices.

Common Questions to Ask When Reviewing the Pipeline

Spending time reviewing the individual sales pipeline reinforces the sales process, and provides a coaching or mentoring opportunity. During the review, the time should be spent discussing the overall health of each individual's pipelines and what they can do to develop it. The focus should be on giving the salespeople actionable items to help them move the deals through the pipeline.

Here are some questions commonly used when reviewing the sales pipeline with salespeople. You can use these as starting points for discussions on the health of the pipeline:

- How many opportunities were won and lost in the period?

Understanding the win/loss ratio helps to determine the success of the sales process and the skill of the salespeople.

- At what stage of the pipeline did the opportunities drop out?

Which stage opportunities drop out of the pipeline will show where the weaknesses of the salespeople are. Is the organization losing out in product features or price? Or perhaps it is the salesperson's presentations that need to be upgraded?

- Are there any opportunities that have been at a stage in the pipeline for a long period?

Stale opportunities show a lack of engagement with the customer. There is a risk that such customers may end up going to a competitor, resulting in a lost sale. If the opportunity is left at a stage by the salesperson, they might have too many accounts in their portfolio. If the customer is stalling, then perhaps a follow up visit is required.

- What is the volume in terms of sales, or revenue, at each stage of the pipeline?

Too low a volume would indicate more leads are necessary. Too large a volume in a stage would suggest that focus might be needed to clear a large deal or a large volume of deals.

Measure the Sales Pipeline Using Metrics

Using metrics to measure the sales pipeline helps to keep things objective, and puts each opportunity into perspective. It allows sales operations to be aware of the possibilities and the challenges that may arise from the deals in the pipeline. These metrics will also form a benchmark for results across salespeople, as well as for future reviews.

These are the metrics commonly used when measuring the health of the pipeline:

- Number of deals in the pipeline
- Average deal size
- Conversion rate - % chance that a deal moves to the next pipeline stage
- Average time spent in each stage of the pipeline

This allows you to understand what a healthy pipeline looks like, and calculate the opportunity to win ratio. Understanding the conversion rates will allow a forecast of how many deals will ultimately close, and how many opportunities in the pipeline are needed to achieve a certain target.

Looking at the average deal size will give an idea when a large deal has entered the pipeline. When such a deal occurs, it will be worth allocating additional resources to developing the deal and ensuring that extra attention is given to the process.

The time spent on each deal will show when an anomaly occurs. Stalling in any stage of the pipeline may indicate that the client is considering offers from competitors, or they have lost focus or lost interest in the deal altogether. In such situations, a salesperson should be sent to follow up with the client and keep the lead warm.

Moving the Deal Forward

Making better decisions in managing the pipeline is the key to keep the deals flowing. To achieve that, sales operations and sales management need to determine what an ideal pipeline should look like, and there needs to be a well defined sales process in place.

Some actions will help in moving deals forward more than others, it is the responsibility of sales operations to conduct the pipeline review, and follow up with sales managers to coach the individual salespeople on this. Here are some examples of how to move deals forward through the pipeline:

1. Guidance or support on the sales stage

   With some deals it may be more tricky to navigate certain parts of the sales process. Whether it's developing the solution, negotiating the deal, or closing the sale, sometimes a salesperson, even an experienced one, may require guidance or support.

2. Gaining access to decision maker

   Sometimes what it takes to move a deal forward is to escalate the negotiations to the management level to gain access to a decision maker. Also known as a buying influence or a sponsor to the sale in some sales methodologies, this is basically the person that signs off on the deal.

   Getting a senior manager or company director in on the negotiations makes it easier to convince the person who is the final decision maker directly!

3. Dropping the client

After putting in time and effort, sometimes it is difficult to let go of a deal or recognize that it is lost. When red flags are present, the best course of action is to drop the client if there is no hope of recovery. While painful, this will save time and effort on the business's part, allowing resources to be better allocated to other deals.

Sales operations will need to work with sales managers to recognize when the above needs to happen to move deals forward, and then work with managers and salespeople alike to make it happen until a point where this can be done on a regular basis with sales managers and their direct reports.

Use Technology

Having a CRM system is helpful in managing your pipeline, and having access to a mobile version of that goes even further in enabling your salespeople.

According to Salesforce.com, a leading CRM systems provider, having a CRM can increase sales by up to 29%, and increase salespeople productivity by up to 34%. Having access to a mobile platform increases total productivity by another 15%.

These figures may look impressive, but know before you invest that a CRM system is a huge commitment in time and effort, and not to mention money as well. A full implementation can take up to a year, and requires constant effort to drive adoption. This is a full project in its own right, and must not be undertaken halfheartedly.

The good news is that it can be integrated to work with your business's sales processes, and a good sales operations function would be enabling the salespeople to adopt these together.

Chapter 6. Enable Your Salespeople to Drive Revenue Up

The purpose of sales enablement is to ensure that the salespeople have access to the necessary knowledge to perform and excel at their jobs. This includes the sales organization's sales tools and other platforms or applications as well. The main areas of sales enablement are in training, content, sales tools, and sales processes; this also includes selecting and adjusting the above to support the organization's sales strategy.

The importance of this has increased in the recent past. According to SiriusDecisions, a B2B research and advisory firm, the spend on sales enablement has doubled in B2B organizations between 2012 and 2014. There has been an increase in 69% in sales enablement technology spending as well during that period.

Setting Up a Sales Enablement Program

Setting up a sales enablement program is an integral part of sales operations. Without an enablement program a lot of the benefit from sales operations does will not be transferred to salespeople.

1. Clearly define the objectives of the program

    A sales enablement program should be targeted at a specific area of sales; from improving a certain stage of the sales process, to better equipping salespeople with knowledge about a product or service, or improving their competency with a   tool.

2. Clearly define the processes needed by the salespeople

Understanding the situation is the first step to solving a problem. To know which processes the salespeople need to learn and understand, find out more about the problem the program is designed to address.

From there the solution can be broken down into steps and made into a process to address the issue.

3. Source for the tools to be used, and integrate them into processes

Sometimes tools may be needed to make a process smoother, or shorten the time taken to complete a task. As an example, CPQ (Configure Price Quote) systems will reduce the time taken to produce complex quotations based upon client requirements. When considering purchasing a tool, the existing tools in the business need to be examined first for potential integration, and it is worth mentioning that tools should be selected based upon a pragmatic approach to the salespeople's needs.

Tools may also be created in-house; from playbooks to catalogues or presentation decks, these are collateral that will help salespeople in the field.

4. Communicate or train the salespeople

Once the above is done, it is necessary to train the salespeople and ensure that the knowledge, the ideals, and the objectives are understood. Adopting a new process takes time, and constant reinforcement may be necessary from regular hands on sessions or reviews to periodical refresher training sessions.

5. Measure, validate, and modify

Once the program is in place, it is important to measure and validate the results   to ensure that it is achieving its intended purpose. If it is not, it may be necessary to modify the process, the training, the tools, or all the above.

The above is a simplified outline of how to develop programs for sales enablement, from mentoring, training, to on-boarding, as well as more complex programs like a roll out of a CRM system, or the adoption of a new sales process. Each of these will have its own intricacies, with its own possible points of success or failure but overall the structure outline above would address a large portion of it for the small business.

Developing a Resource Library for Sales

As sales develops, it is common to have a collection of material from training manuals, product catalogues, templates, presentation decks, and other documents used in sales. However a report by International Data Corporation (IDC), a provider of market intelligence, advisory services and events, found that up to 80% of content is not used. This could be due to three possible issues according to IDC:

1. Salespeople are not aware that the content exists
2. Salespeople do not have time to look for the content
3. The amount of content is overwhelming to go through

These issues stem from a lack of organization around collateral, and can be solved by creating a resource library.

It is important for sales operations to take the lead and manage the library so that there is control over the quality of the content, consistency in messaging, and easy access to the material.

A good practice is to categorize the information, breaking down the material by topics, document type, and which stage of the sales process it is needed. In this way, the information is easily searchable by anyone who is looking for it.

Chapter 7. Measuring Your Success

It has been said that without analysis, any hypothesis is just another opinion.

You also cannot improve what you do not measure, hence it is the use of data that allows companies to make informed decisions and take an objective view on sales. This will allow the business to optimize the utilization of resources such as time, money, and manpower. Furthermore, sales analysis is also crucial for understanding the customer, defining the right product mix, and other assessing other business objectives.

Key Performance Indicators

It is a common belief that the only indicator of success in a sales team is the actual sales, and that the value of a sales representative is his or her production. Certainly, this is at the core of any business, however sales is a form of a lagging indicator meaning that it is an evaluation of past performance.

If a sales representative has no sales today, it is an indication that the team may not be adhering to the recommended sales activities for months. Sales operations should be looking at the pipeline, and considering that in the monthly projections as this indicates the sales process may not have been followed which would cause difficulty in closing the deal later on.

Key Performance Indicators (KPIs) are crucial indicators to ensure that the sales department has a robust pipeline for sales. KPIs can provide an objective platform to measure activities and allow a glimpse into the future.

Important KPIs that You Must Monitor Regularly

Sales is a numbers game, and the capacity to analyze the right metrics is the best justification for the sales operations team. While sales management is also based on human behavior, the ultimate measurement of the team's success is on the sales figures. Below are the top sales KPIs that should be monitored:

Number of New Prospects / Leads per Month

This KPI significantly depends on the nature of business. New prospects could be people who subscribed to a newsletter or received a product trials. They may also be new visitors on the organization website and spent a particular length of time without buying anything.

It is important to define the new prospects figure to make sure that the data about the number of new prospective clients is accurate. This KPI is valuable in sales analysis, but mainly it can help you determine if the monthly marketing spend is justifiable.

Number of New Customers per Month

The best way to measure the success of a sales campaign is to look into the sales results per month. The conversion for KPI will show how many new clients purchased products or signed up for services in a month.

This KPI should be expressed as both a figure of monthly sales, and as a percentage of the monthly sales quota to determine if the team can achieve it's annual sales target. Additionally, to determine what is causing an increase or decrease in a metric, the correlation between marketing processes and sales campaigns should be more carefully analyzed.

A comparative analysis to study the monthly sales KPIs with the results of the past month can be done to check if the sales figure is rising or plummeting. This is important to spot the root cause of poor results. Common causes of slow sales progress include:

- unqualified or under qualified leads from marketing calls
- non-performing sales representatives
- lean seasons

Furthermore, by monitoring the number of monthly new leads so projections can be made on the possible number of closed sales in a given period.

Finally it should be noted that many of the sales metrics may overlap with the KPIs defined by the marketing team.

Cost Per Lead

All parts of sales activities to entice new customers will cost money. This includes social media management, web design, and advertising expenses. These activities, effective or not effective, will take a considerable amount of money.

The cost per lead KPI should be included in all analysis to measure how much it will cost to acquire new potential clients. The cost per lead can be calculated by the sum of all marketing expenses in a month, and dividing it by the number of new leads in the month.

In order to obtain accurate KPIs which reflect the real scenario, large amounts of data are needed. The fastest way to gather data into a single system is to use a software that is able to employ all the data available for comprehensive reporting as well as updated KPI monitors.

A plummeting cost per lead could be a sign of enhanced customer experience or better brand awareness. On the other hand, a rising cost per lead may indicate the need to review the marketing strategy and concentrate on channels that are more profitable.

Lead-Sale Conversion Percentage

Lead-Sale Conversion Rate refers to the percentage of new customers in comparison to new prospective customers. This KPI will show if the sales team has the capacity of converting prospective deals into actual business. For example, if only 5 per cent of new leads are converted into actual customers, 95 per cent of leads are lost leads.

Sales operations should also provide recommendations to improve KPIs. For example, one way to improve the Lead-Sale Conversion Rate is to create better marketing and sales collaterals and provide better benefits for the prospect customers. Discounts and promotions, or better customer experience throughout the sales process are also viable alternatives. There are many reasons why a business may lose leads. Sales operations can help the business figure out these specific causes and enhance the sales results by identifying areas of concern.

Cost Per Conversion

It is a common misconception that Cost per Conversion is similar to Cost per Lead. However it must be noted that Cost per Conversion is on a higher tier of value as compared to Cost per Lead, as only a small number of leads can be converted to actual customers or subscribers. Hence, the cost for one conversion could be significantly higher.

Take note that the cost per conversion is computed as cost per lead, divided by the number of new sales or customers for the month.

To take a look if the Cost per Conversion is valuable in the long-term, Customer Lifetime Value (CLV) should be considered. When the cost per conversion is quite high that the CLV comes out negative, the organization might be losing money and management needs to act quickly to improve profit margins.

Customer Lifetime Value (CLV)

CLV refers to the revenue that the business can make from providing services to a customer for a particular length of time. This metric can be obtained by combining the profit earned as well as the cost spent related to nurturing and maintaining the relationship with that customer.

In sales analysis, this KPI will shows the worth of a customer to the business. If the company is spending more money in converting a lead into a paying customer than the customer spends on products by the business, maybe it is time to review the business strategy.

Furthermore, the client profitability measurement can be employed to compute the profitability of various customer groups. This can also be segregated by creating different client categories based on user groups as well as buyer personas based on industry, interests, location, and age to get the CLV by segment.

The CLV of all customer categories can also be analyzed to better understand segments that are bringing in higher returns. It may be a strategy for the business to consider letting go of customers who are not contributing to the net profit or are also difficult to convert.

Take note that the best way to increase customer profitability is to extend the average CLV by building loyalty.

Net Promoter Score

This KPI will show the probability that a customer may recommend the company's products or services to others. This data can be analyzed from interviews and customer surveys. The best way to gather this data is to ask questions in the follow-up messages from new subscriptions or new purchases.

Basically, there are three tiers of customer advocacy:

- Detractors (Score 0 to 6). These are unhappy clients who may share negative feedback about your company and may affect your image.
- Passives (Score 7 to 8). These are satisfied clients who are more likely to jump ship when they see better offers.
- Promoters (Score 9 to 10). These are raving fans who are willing to share positive feedback about the company and may affect the image positively.

To obtain this KPI, subtract the percentage of Detractors from the percentage of Promoters. During the analysis phase, compare the customer success metrics through several months to check the progress of the customer experience over time. A falling Net Promoter Score may indicate the presence of a strong competitor and is now poaching clients from the organization.

Online Conversion Rate

Most businesses nowadays have websites, which helps the company to promote its brand through aesthetics, easy user experience, and appropriate brand colors. The online conversion rate will show the percentage of visitors who perform an action on the company's website. This is crucial in reviewing the online marketing strategies that the company is implementing.

Customer Attrition Rate

The customer attrition rate is also known as customer turnover rate. This KPI shows how many clients decide to cancel their subscription or buying products from the business. For sustainable business growth, the number of new sales must surpass the churn rate.

This KPI is obtained by getting the percentage of customers who have cancelled their relationship with the business during the past year. For instance, if 10 customers out of 100 cancels their subscription, then the attrition rate is 10%. It is valuable to track this metric over time, to understand when an anomaly occurs. For example, if the usual attrition rate is 10% a month and it increases to 25% action should be taken to find out why; this could be the result of competition or changes in the market.

Also, it is important to differentiate between involuntary attrition or voluntary attrition. Involuntary attrition occurs if the decision of the customer is caused by bankruptcy or relocation and they are not capable of continuing the relationship with the business. On the other hand, voluntary attrition happens if the customer finds another provider because they think they are getting a better deal.

In order to maintain a low attrition rate, the business should provide outstanding customer care as well as user experience and strive to be ahead of the competition.

Chapter 8. Forecasting Future Performance

Sales operations are essential in producing reports and analysis which drive recommendations. By using predictive models, the sales operations department can help take an active role in closing the gap between expected and actual sales performance.

Accurate sales forecasts allow companies to make informed business decisions, such as product launches, headcount needs, cash flow, and other resource allocations.

As the business expands, sales forecasting becomes a more important benchmark for the health of the company. It is easy to measure the success of a business by looking at its batting average on hitting its sales forecasts. If the business projects high sales in the 3rd quarter but only achieved 50% profitability, this is an indicator that the business is performing poorly and the management has no understanding of its capacity to hit sales targets. In attracting new investors for private businesses, sales forecasting could be used to project the possible ROI.

With accurate sales forecasting, a business can benefit from high efficiency, cost savings, increased profits and better customer service.

Generating Sales Forecasts

It is actually easy to make a sales forecast. The challenging part is sustaining the comprehensive and genuine financial records required to support the math. In making a sales forecast, you need to consider factors like:

1. number of sales that are canceled
2. returned sales for each product broken down by month, and
3. external factors affecting sales like:

   - economic forecasts – fluctuations in the economy may affect buyer sentiments
   - price fluctuations in raw materials – the price of raw materials will affect your costing for your products and services
   - more competitors - more competitors may push your company to offer price cuts and slashed profits

The easiest sales forecast to make is the yearly sales forecast. If the business achieved stability, which means there are no problems with the employees or the customers, then it only requires inflation. Below is the formula:

Annual sales last year + (sales last year x inflation rate) = sales forecast for the next year

This is usually further adjusted for sales effort, expected RFPs, and other factors (such as the attrition of existing customers).

Seasonal variation

For most businesses, sales could fluctuate with varying seasons. If this is the case, then it is possible to organize the sales forecast each month. The first thing that needs to be done is to assess the previous years of sales number to obtain the percentage of the total sales for the year.

For example, in the first quarter, the organization may make 5% of the total annual sales, but in the second quarter, it can make 15%. This data can be used to project the total sales for the year, regardless if it is the low season or high season by using the present monthly sales number.

If it is March and the sales figures for February are available, the forecast for the rest of the year can be made because the first quarter accounts for 5% of the yearly total sales.

It is uncommon for a business to experience stable sales every year even with seasonal consideration. In calculating the sales forecasts, other factors need to be considered. Examples of such are sales contracts that will not be renewed, new sales contracts, projections for growth, projection for trend in the consumer buying power, and political trends that may affect the customers.

It can be challenging to create a sales forecast for a new business with no previous record of sales. In this phase, sales forecasts are crucial for enticing investors and qualifying for financing. The standard method for computing the sales forecast for a new business is to refer the prediction on the performance of similar companies that are offering similar products or services.

It is crucial to base the forecast on companies that are catering to the same customer demographic and are operating in the same location. For retail, it is important to figure out the average annual or monthly sales volume for every square foot of space. With this, it is possible to become more flexible for the relative size of the store.

Qualitative data may be collected by visiting competitors, talking to their customers and sales representatives. This help build profile of the organization's target market. With survey data, it is possible to find out the number of people in each area that fits the company's customer profile and use this data in projecting sales.

Top Down Approach Vs. Bottom Up Approach in Sales Forecasting

Top down and bottom up approaches are applicable not only in business but also in economics and finance. Top down refers to the process of analysis from the general to the specific, while bottom up refers to the process of assessment from the specific to the general.

Top Down Sales Forecasting

This analytical process begins with the general perspective. It starts with the industry projections and trickles down to the business, departments, individuals, and products.

In a top down approach for sales forecasting, begin with the market capitalization for the industry, then break it down by product lines and formats. Understanding the market share of the business will help in estimating how long it may take to achieve its goal. This will determine which resources sales would need to invest in to be successful in capturing market share.

Sales projections becomes more accurate as the amount of industry data accessible increases. It is crucial that to use as much available information as possible to ensure that any sales forecasts made will be more accurate. Market patterns and trends are much easier to spot on if the demand and supply factors are similar for certain geographic areas and products. This system is also beneficial for new businesses if there are no sales records yet.

For budgeting, aggregate budgets are calculated through industry best practices as well as guidelines. These are then assigned to specific departments and finally to certain products and services.

The main concern with using the top down approach in sales forecasting is that the regions and the products are mixed. This may result to the average low and high numbers in the final sales analysis report. The estimates may not accurately represent any particular product or area. Hence, there can be a generalization for patterns and trends.

Bottom Up Sales Forecasting

The primary benefit of using bottom up approach in sales forecasting is it concentrates the attention on the assumptions underlying certain sales, expenses, and profit points for every product or service. Sales managers and sales analysts are much involved in this approach compared to the top down method.

The bottom up approach is also helpful for setting objectives for sales, production and hiring especially for assigning resources to certain items to achieve sales goals. Sales forecasting tend to be more precise for companies with seasonal sales cycle or businesses who often experience fluctuations in their gross sales and net profits.

One of the major downsides of using the bottom up approach in sales forecasting is that the mistakes at the micro level can be amplified as they move towards the macro level. These are then compounded during the process of expansion.

Hybrid Method to Improve Accuracy in Sales Forecasting

The last of the approaches is the hybrid approach of the bottom up and top down models. The goal here is to highlight the benefits of using both systems while minimizing the downsides that could result to more accurate projections. Using the two methods can also serve as a check and balance system for sales forecasting.

Using the hybrid approach is ideal if there is not enough industry data to work with and if the sales team tend to underestimate or overestimate their production objectives. The differences in the projections are reviewed so more reliable results are obtained.

Remember, forecasting is crucial for decision making and proper business planning. This is needed for cash flow monitoring, assessing break-even points, evaluating the capacity of the business to pay back its debt, getting external financing, and increasing net profits. The approaches may range from educated projections to complex mathematical calculations.

Both approaches have their own advantages and disadvantages. Hybrid methods are employed to amplify the benefits and avoid the downsides to improve the dependability for each approach.

Conclusion

Thank you for taking the time to read this book!

I hope that you have gained an understanding of how sales operations can benefit your business. If you enjoyed this book, please take the time to leave me a review on Amazon. I appreciate your honest feedback, and it really helps me to continue producing high quality books.